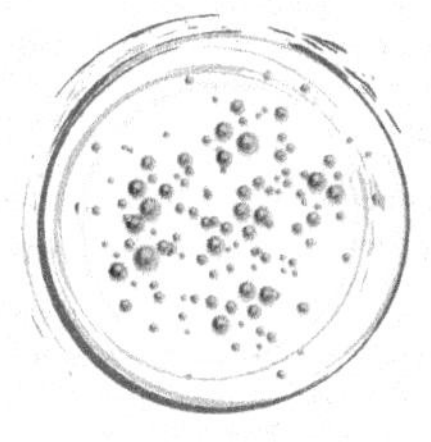

SHI BAN GONG BEI

*Seventy-Seven Pearls
of Business Wisdom*

MING WANG
HARVARD & MIT (MD);
PhD (Laser Physics)

ATTRIBUTIONS
Interior Text Font: Minion Pro
Cover Design & Typesetting: Robbie W. Grayson III

BOOK PUBLISHER INFORMATION
Traitmarker Books
A Division of Traitmarker Media, LLC
www.traitmarkerbooks.com
traitmarker@gmail.com
ISBN | 979-8-8691-9294-3

Table of Contents

A Note

Introduction

Shi Ban Gong Bei is an ancient Chinese saying about accomplishing twice the work in half the time. If you begin anything with the right perspective, you make your life easier. As an eye doctor, I know how important clear physical sight is in my patients' lives.

I also know how important clear moral and logical sight can be to people's lives. Living in tune with the truth of who people are and how the world works can save you untold trouble. Living out of tune with those truths can feel as frustrating as trying to cut a steak with a spoon.

Through my travel, education, and daily work with people, I have gathered the following pearls of wisdom. I offer them to you here in the hope that they will ease your way through life. I hope that using them will lend you the clear spiritual sight that I prize above anything else.

Ming Wang | Nashville

TRAITMARKER MEDIA

SHI BAN GONG BEI

事半功倍

*Seventy-Seven Pearls
of Business Wisdom*

*(Combining the Wisdom of the East
and the West to Accomplish Things
More Successfully and Efficiently)*

MING WANG

HARVARD & MIT (MD);
PHD (Laser Physics)

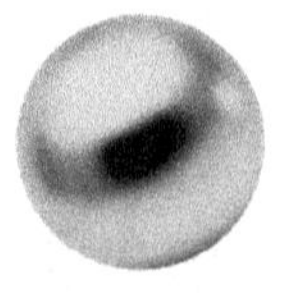

Pearl 1

*In partnership,
the person is more
important than
the project.*

In partnership, who your partner *is* is more important than
what you will be doing together.
Examine the character of a poten-
tial partner before entering into a
business relationship with them.
With the right partner, you may
be able to do the right thing. However, with the wrong partner, you
may *never* be able to do the right
thing.

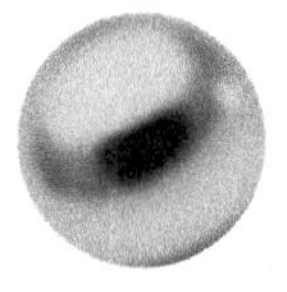

PEARL 2

*In solving a problem,
the matter is more
important than
the person.*

When addressing a problem, you should not focus on the personal attributes of the individual who made the mistake. If you do, you will place the focus on the person, which may incite their ego and create an emotional barrier that could cause them never to be able to see the issue itself. Therefore, you should focus on the issue instead of the person. The goal is to solve the problem and improve the system, not to blame a particular person.

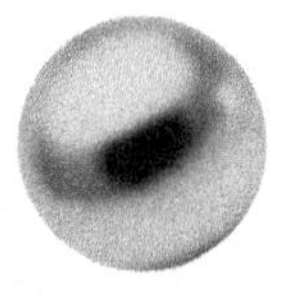

Pearl 3

*Life is a
two-way street.*

If you need someone to assist you with your project, you *first* need to do everything you can to help that person with *their* project. Then they will be more inclined to help you with yours. A person who always wants to take but never give will *never* be successful.

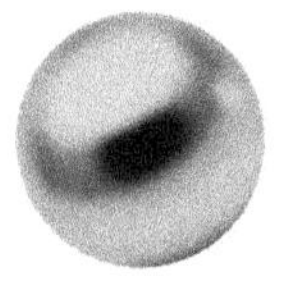

Pearl 4

*Make it
easy for others
to help you.*

If you need help with your project,
you need to first accomplish as
much of it as you can yourself. Don't
be lazy. If the person from whom
you need help sees that you truly
care about your own project and
that you have already done as much
of it as you can yourself before you
ask for help, they will be more willing to assist you. Furthermore, the
more you have done yourself prior
to asking for help, the less they will
have to do, so the easier it will be for
them to help you.

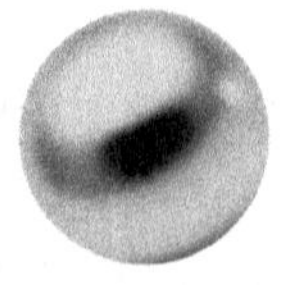

PEARL 5

*Why am
I here
today?*

Whatever you are doing, *always* be willing to step back for a moment, look at the whole situation, and ask yourself this key question—"Ultimately, what is the real reason or purpose of me being here today?"

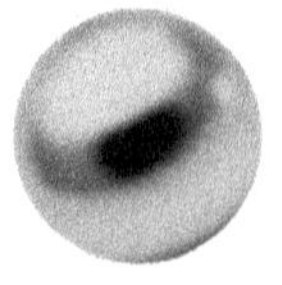

PEARL 6

*Identify the
#1 task.*

When faced with many chal-
lenges, *rank* them in order of
importance so you can devote *most*
of your attention to the #1 task. The
ability to rank is at the core of the
human experience!

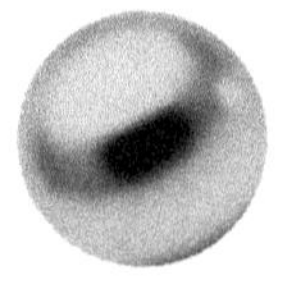

PEARL 7

*Apply logic
to everything
you do.*

Apply logic to everything you do—whether it is big or small—and ask yourself two questions: "Does it actually make logical sense?" and "How can I solve this problem more logistically?"

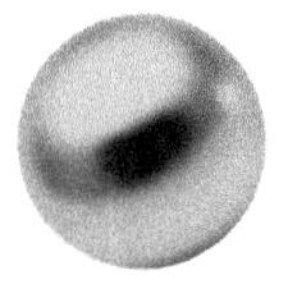

Pearl 8

*Check things
orthogonally.*

When you check something for accuracy, try *not* to use the same method that you used to obtain your initial result. Because if there was an error with that method, you would likely make the same mistake again! You are much more likely to catch an error if you use a completely different and unrelated—i.e., orthogonal ("in logic")—method the second time.

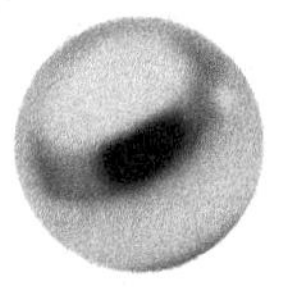

Pearl 9

Focus on content
before form.

C ontent is *more* important than form, and substance is *much* *more* important than formality.

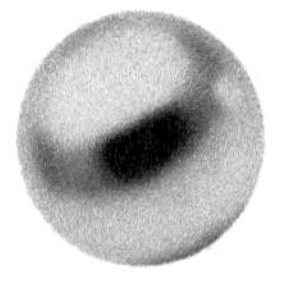

Pearl 10

*Focus only
on what you do
and the things
you can control.*

Don't worry about what others do. Focus *only* on what you yourself can do. Do not waste any time on things that are not under your control. Focus *only* on things you *can* do or change.

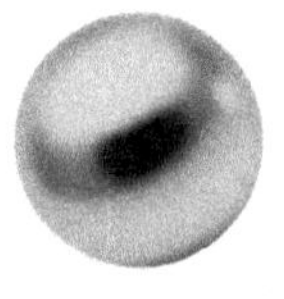

PEARL 11

*Learn from
the mistakes
of others.*

Learn from the mistakes of others, so, hopefully, you won't have to make the same mistakes yourself.

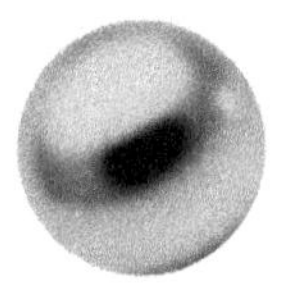

Pearl 12

*Stay focused
on the point.*

Don't be distracted by examples that people use. Aways keep your focus on the issue itself.

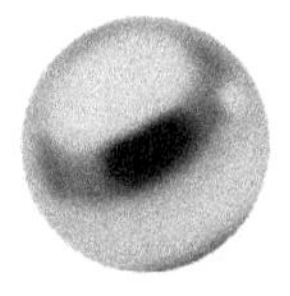

Pearl 13

*Don't try
to change someone else.
Adapt and change
yourself.*

You cannot change another person anyway, but you can change yourself. Your ideal work partner should be someone who—at the onset—already possesses many attributes that will enable you to work well together. If adjustments are needed after you begin working together, adapt and change yourself.

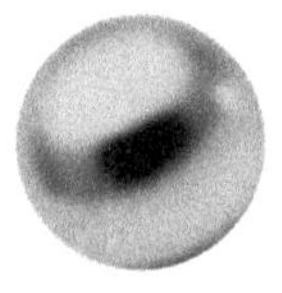

Pearl 14

*Success is
measured by effort,
not by the result.*

Success is *not* defined by how much we have accomplished but by whether or not we have made our *best* effort. If you have done your best in everything you have done, then you are successful!

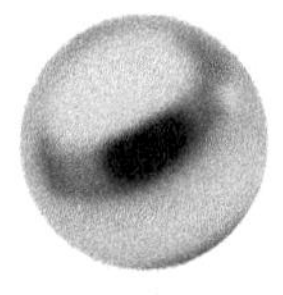

Pearl 15

*People will do
what others have done
in a similar situation.*

If you want someone to do something, first try to identify and
then convey to them what others in
a similar situation previously have
done since people generally feel
more comfortable doing something
that has been done by others who
have been in their shoes.

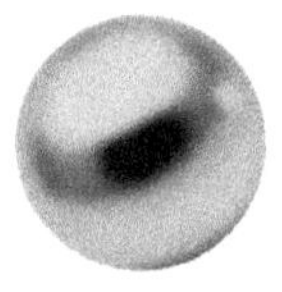

Pearl 16

*Can I do this
a bit better?*

Whatever you are part of—
whether it is a process or a
product—always be willing to ask
yourself, "Can I do this *a bit* better?"

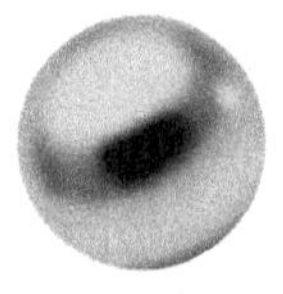

PEARL 17

*Help others
to recall
the issue first.*

When you follow up with
someone on an issue, re-
member that—although you are
fully aware of it (since it is your
issue)—they may *not* be! So, first,
try to help the person recall what
it is all about so they won't have to
spend *extra* time themselves figuring
that out. If the individual has to do
that, they may very well end up *not*
doing the things you want them to
do because it seems like it would be
just too much trouble. And it is *not*
even their project to begin with!

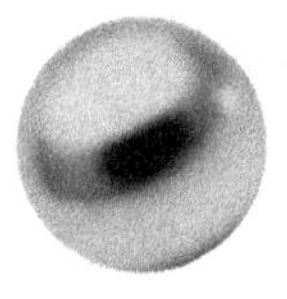

Pearl 18

*Always
be prepared
with a back-up plan.*

Whatever you do, go into it
fully prepared with at least
a "plan B"—and sometimes even
a "plan C." When something un-
expected happens and you are not
already prepared with an alternative
plan, going "back to the drawing
board" is a total waste of time!

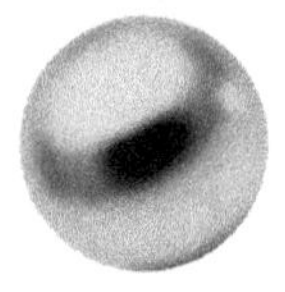

Pearl 19

*Improve
the system
itself.*

When solving a problem, don't be satisfied with only solving the problem itself. Instead, try to examine *the system* from which the problem arose in the first place and find ways to improve the underlying system itself.

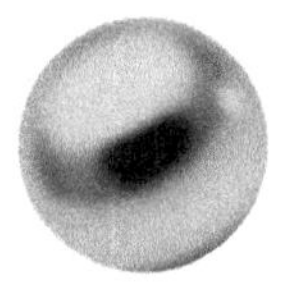

Pearl 20

*Identify
the real intention
of a person.*

The real intention of a drunk-
ard is not necessarily in the
wine. Someone may appear to want
something, but they may *really* want
something else.

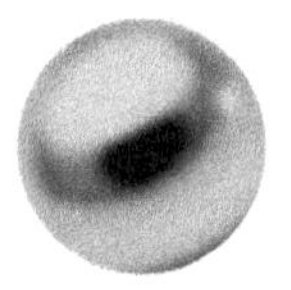

PEARL 21

Listen,
then speak.

Listen first, let people finish what they are saying, and *then* speak. If you wait, you will avoid speaking prematurely.

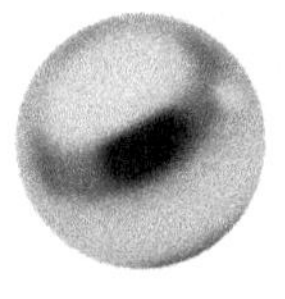

PEARL 22

*Among life's uncertainties,
identify the few things
that are, indeed, certain.*

When faced with many un-
certainties, identify among
them the few things that *are* indeed
certain, and then hang your hat on
them.

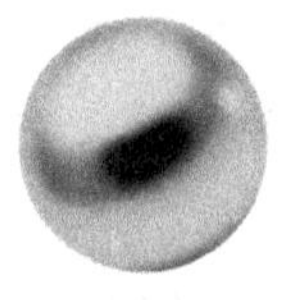

PEARL 23

At least try.

If you don't even try, you have zero chance to succeed. But if you try—even when you only have a 1% chance—it is still much better than the zero!

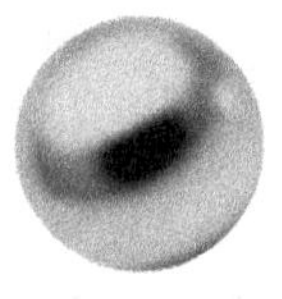

Pearl 24

*There are three criteria
to determine if you do
need to solve a problem.*

Does the problem indeed exist? Is it actually a big enough problem to merit the time and effort that it will take to solve it? Will solving it *really* matter?

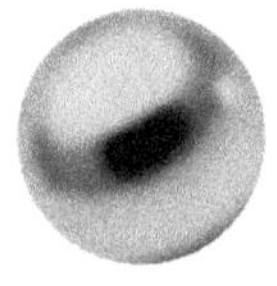

Pearl 25

*On what does
human happiness
depend?*

It is not how much you have or how much you want that determines your happiness in life. Human happiness depends on the distance between *how much* you have and *how much* you want. The smaller that distance is, the happier you are.

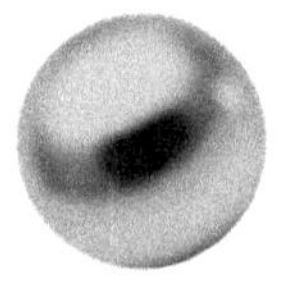

Pearl 26

*Restate
the question,
please.*

Before we hurry to answer a question, sometimes it is helpful to ask, "Could you please restate the question again?" Clarifying what has actually been asked of you is often *half* the battle.

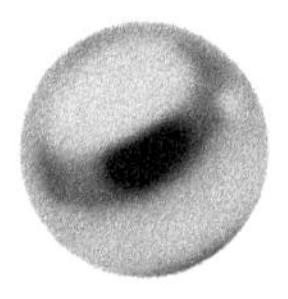

Pearl 27

The goal of life
is to live.

The goal of life is not about
seeing how much we can accomplish but about whether we are happy throughout the journey. Life is not about feeling that we have "arrived" at wherever. It is about enjoying the *process* of trying to get there.

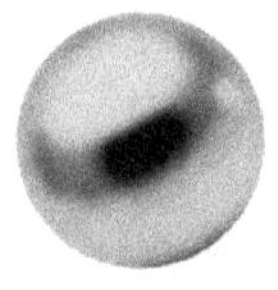

PEARL 28

*You can actually
change the reality
around you.*

The traditional wisdom that you can't really change your surroundings and the reality around you is actually wrong. In fact, you *can!* If you are always positive, always choosing to try to do something rather than not trying at all, always deciding to look at the glass as half full rather than half empty, then eventually you will find that the people around you have all somehow magically *changed* and *now* are all happy! How did your surroundings change like this? Well, this is because *you* have caused it to change! You have chosen to be positive, and you are actually the one who has *created* a similarly happy reality and environment around you! You *can* change it if you so choose. Your subjective choice *does* influence the objective reality around you!

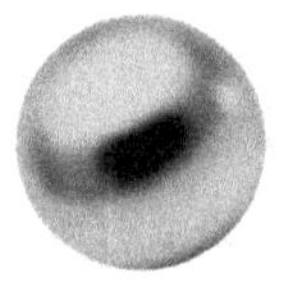

Pearl 29

*Do everything
a little better.*

Contrary to popular belief, people who are successful in life often do *not* have incredible, earth-shattering, unique skills and/or secrets that others don't have. They are just slightly more diligent and alert: always watching with everything they do to try to find opportunities to *maximize* their efforts in order to do a little bit better than others. They may do just 1% better than others in one thing, but cumulatively, they eventually end up doing much better in life overall than most of us.

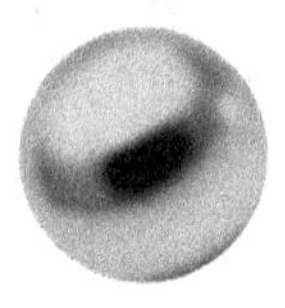

Pearl 30

*90%
of what we think
is happening to us
is actually our
reaction to it.*

Of all the things we think are happening to us, 10% is indeed the things that happen to us over which we have no control. But 90% is actually our reaction over which we *do* have control. So, if we can modify or improve our subjective reaction, we can, in fact, overcome and control 90% of what we believe are objective things that are happening to us.

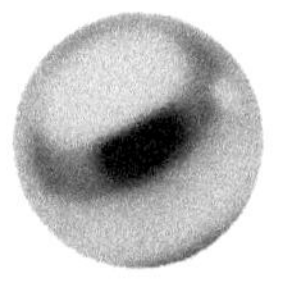

PEARL 31

Yin
and Yang.

Life is about balance: yin and yang. Going to one extreme often generates exactly the opposite effect of what you desire. If you are extreme in your efforts at something, you can actually end up being non-productive and bad at accomplishing the desired goal.

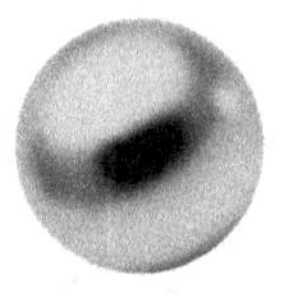

PEARL 32

*Before you speak,
first rank your questions
or answers.*

People pay the most attention to what you say *first*. So before you ask or answer a question, first think it through in your own mind and then ask the most important question first. Similarly, when answering a question, figure out your top and most critical answer and state that first.

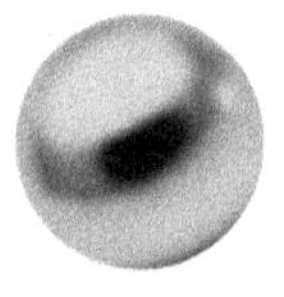

PEARL 33

*A frog at the bottom
of the well does not
see the horizon.*

Each of us is a "frog at the bottom of a well." That is to say, our perspective, basis for judgment, and opinions are limited by our own experience and exposure. We look up and see a small round patch of clear sky and believe it is a beautiful day! However, when we climb out of the well up to ground level and are now able to look around at the *entire* sky, we may realize it is actually a cloudy day! We see that the small patch of sky that we were able to see earlier when we were at the bottom of the well was actually *not at all* representative of the whole situation!

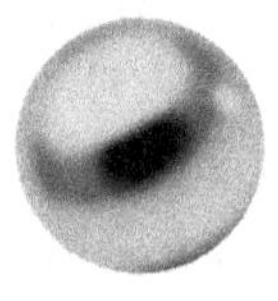

Pearl 34

*The goal of our
communication
is understanding.*

The *goal* of our communication should *not* be to get a chance to just talk! The goal should be to make sure that our listener(s) understand what we are talking about. Don't just continue talking and be oblivious to whether or not your listener understands or even cares at all about what you are saying!

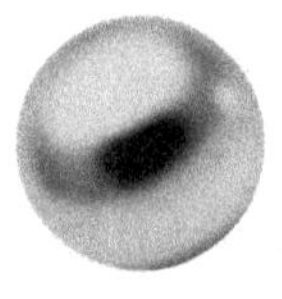

Pearl 35

*Every student
has a best
teacher.*

The best teacher is not someone
who knows the most but rather someone who knows the most
about what their students know.

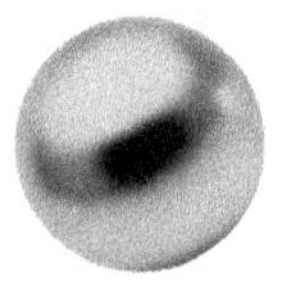

Pearl 36

People may be wrong,
but they still want
to be respected
and heard.

A lthough people may be wrong,
they still want to be respected
and heard, so respect them and let
them fully express their opinion.
Consider carefully what they say.

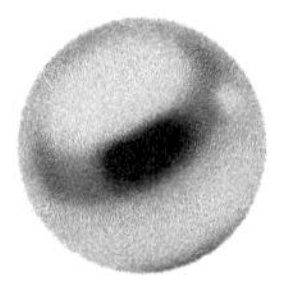

Pearl 37

*Left and right brains—
1+1>2!*

A right-brain dominant person is supposed to be creative and artistic, and one who is considered a left-brain is rational and logical. However, we should not be limited by these classifications (e.g.)—"I am a right-brain person, so I am not good at logical things." Instead, engage your right brain to help you with logical tasks, such as applying artistry to precision eye surgery, and summon your left brain to help your creative work, such as applying me-chanical and physics principles in learning ballroom dancing. Rather than treating them as two isolated halves, our right and left brains are meant to work *together,* synergistical-ly. It is a situation where 1+1 equals actually *more* than 2!

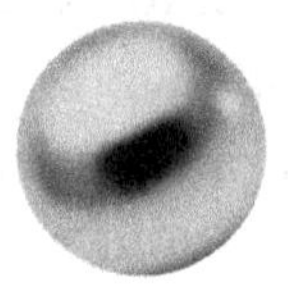

Pearl 38

Don't do it,
don't write it.

If you don't want people to know
what you are doing, then simply
don't do it. And if you don't want
people to read what you have writ-
ten, then *don't* write it!

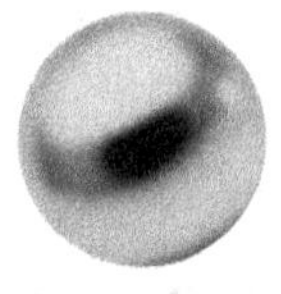

PEARL 39

*Don't criticize
unless you have
a better idea.*

If you don't have a better idea, then keep your mouth closed. If you want to criticize something, always be ready to offer what you believe is a better solution.

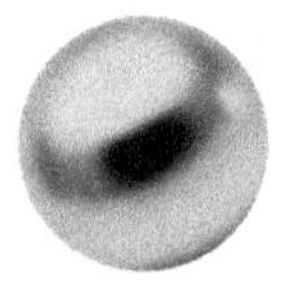

Pearl 40

*The ultimate
drive in life
is love.*

The ultimate drive in life is to *love* what you do! If you don't, then change what you do!

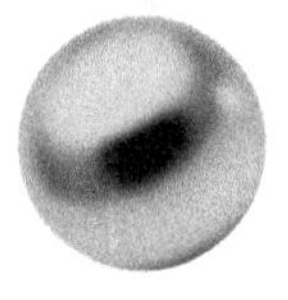

PEARL 41

Maintain fairness,
independent of
human bias
and favoritism.

A system is truly fair if it is independent of the identity of any particular person who is placed in that position or system.

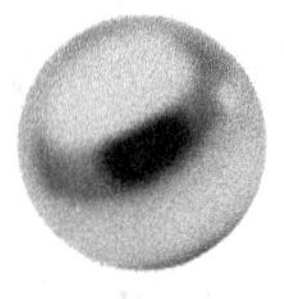

PEARL 42

*Blindness to reality
is the ultimate
failure.*

A human being, if left to their own devices, is bound to become corrupt since we are all selfish by nature. The best way to develop a solid, incorruptible system is *not* to rely upon any assumptions of the goodness or unselfishness of any human being. It should be a fair system, and no one should be above that system.

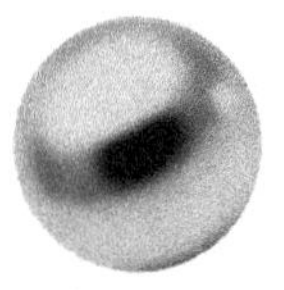

Pearl 43

*Today
is important
too!*

Yesterday is what we have done. Tomorrow is what we will do. But how about today? Should today merely just serve to remember what we did yesterday and prepare for what we will do tomorrow? That is not fair! Today has the right to be its own day! Focus on today, stay in the moment, and make the best of right now! Think about it: the reason that we actually need to constantly remind ourselves as such is because we naturally really *don't* do this. Instead, we tend to focus only on the past or future and ignore today!

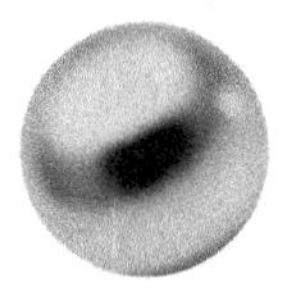

PEARL 44

*Make a deal
you would be happy
to accept.*

A truly fair business deal is one in which you can picture yourself stepping into your partner's shoes— and when you look at the deal from that perspective, it is still fair. In all human interactions, always be willing to look at things from the other's prospective.

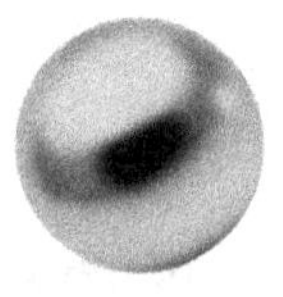

Pearl 45

*Establish validity
before you examine
efficacy.*

If Johnny always tells lies, you are not going to listen to anything that he says! So before you consider what a person has to say, first spend some time examining their validity. Only evaluate what a person actually says *after* you have the chance to first establish that they are indeed reliable and that their opinion (whatever it is) is indeed worth considering.

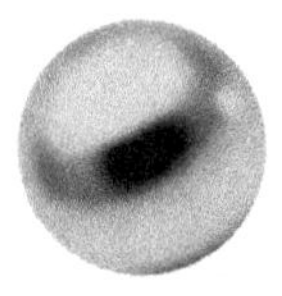

Pearl 46

*Never assume
that you are
the smartest person
in the world.*

If people do something in a different way than you do it, don't just
dismiss their way, believing you are
a smarter person. You *will* be proven
wrong! People do things in certain
ways for a reason. It is better to be
humble and study what they do and
why they do it, as there is always
something to learn from everyone.

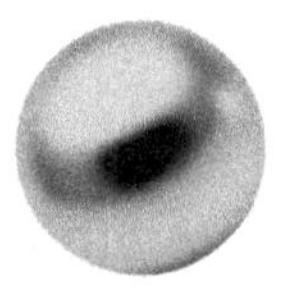

PEARL 47

*Start with
the big picture.*

You can't see the forest for the trees." So always start with the big picture (the "forest") before being bogged down with individual details (the "trees").

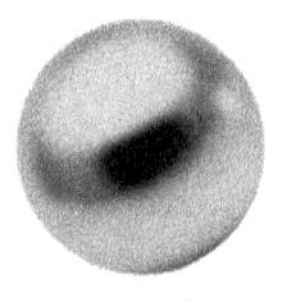

PEARL 48

*Kill many birds
with one stone.*

The best way to improve efficien-
cy is to identify the commonal-
ities among the tasks that you need
to do, and try to do just one (or very
few) thing(s) that will take care of
everything.

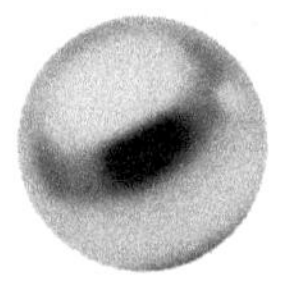

PEARL 49

*Improve the method
of how something
is done.*

9 9% of us focus on accomplishing a job, but only 1% do more than that. After a job is done, 99% will move on to other things, but the 1% linger a bit longer, ponder and reflect, "Can I do this sort of thing a bit better the next time around? Has another person finished this job in a way that was actually better than mine? What can I learn from this experience so I can improve the way I do things in the future?" The nature of the work that we do will not stay with us (since we will do different things tomorrow), but, the improvements in our method of doing things, which are made by learning from this experience, *will* indeed *stay* with us and will benefit us in the future.

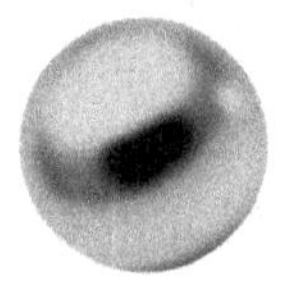

Pearl 50

To be successful
is to work
selectively.

People say that in order to be successful, one has to be talented and work hard. While these two factors are indeed two of the top three qualities needed to be successful, however, *neither* is actually the #1! The most important thing to do if you want to be successful is to work intelligently by selecting only a few things, focusing on them, and doing the best you can with those few things. The goal is not to continue adding to your to-do list, but rather to work on subtracting various things on your plate until there is actually nothing left to subtract.

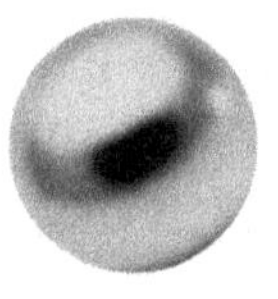

Pearl 51

*Maximal alignment
means minimal work.*

In a business collaboration, maximal alignment of interests in the beginning produces minimal work later. The opposite is also true: minimal alignment of interests among the various parties early on often ends up necessitating a lot of unproductive work later.

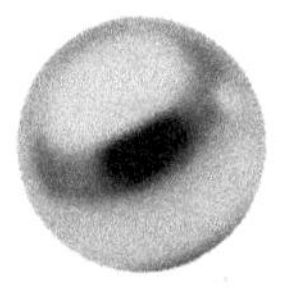

Pearl 52

*Clearly define
the issue first.*

When you clearly define the issue first, you are actually already halfway there!

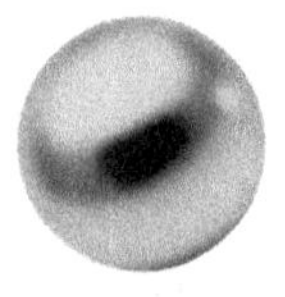

Pearl 53

*Fiduciary
responsibilities
cover both parties.*

The fiduciary responsibility of a leader is to listen to and carefully consider a team member's suggestion. The fiduciary responsibility of a team member is to accept a leader's final decision and do it!

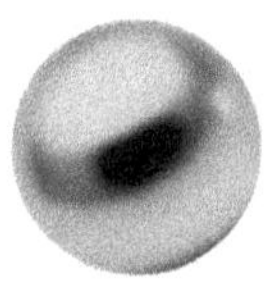

Pearl 54

*More important
than doing things is
learning how to behave
while doing them.*

While what we do changes over time, how we do things, as well as our human quality and attributes that are reflected through the things we do and how we do it, does *not* change. For example, do we do what we have promised? Are we good communicators? Do we know life is a "two-way street"?

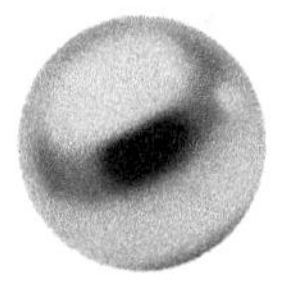

Pearl 55

*A proud person
eats what
is bitter.*

If the things we do don't turn out
how we had hoped they would,
yet the decision to do them was our
own to begin with, then we as human beings tend to be more accept-
ing of the outcome than we would
have been if the decision to do them
was made for us by others. The
reason for this is that in the former
situation, we have no one to blame
but ourselves.

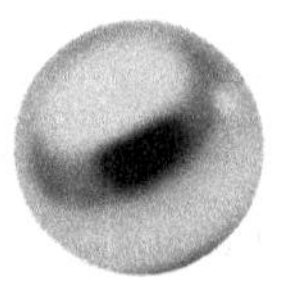

Pearl 56

*You can
make yourself
happier.*

Human beings become unhappy when we unwisely compare what we have with the ideal and often non-existent alternatives! So, the way to make ourselves happier—which *does* work every time—is to compare your current situation *only* with other *existing* alternatives. As long as your current situation is better than all other existing alternatives, you will be happy!

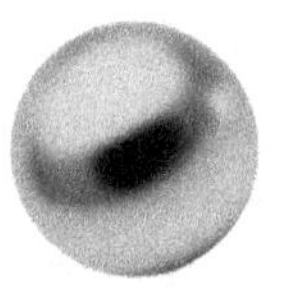

Pearl 57

*Pick
the longest straw
you see.*

We sometimes are stuck in inaction because we feel that the method that we have is still not the perfect one. Well, the 100% ideal method actually does *not* exist! So, as long as what we are considering is the best among the existing choices of method, then let's do it! Ideal height does not really exist at all. Life is about picking the longest straw.

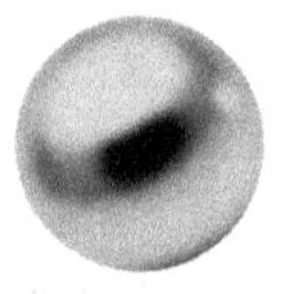

Pearl 58

*Two references
provide double
security.*

For important things, always use "double security" measures. For example, in communication, use BOTH the date and the day of the week, since our chance of making mistakes for BOTH is very slim.

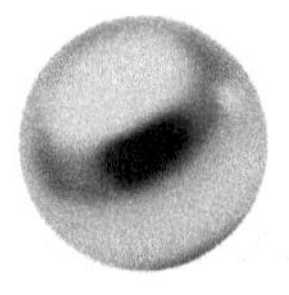

PEARL 59

*Focus on
improving
yourself.*

Some people live by focusing on [the errors of] others or even by trying to sabotage others (e.g., a competitor). A *much better* and productive way of living, however, is to focus on *yourself* (i.e., how to improve *yourself*).

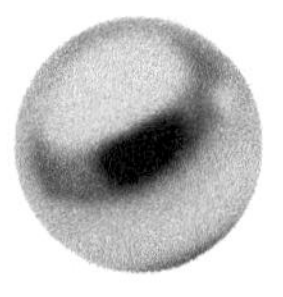

Pearl 60

*While in
safety, think
of danger.*

Even when things are going well, don't become complacent. Think of things that could go wrong. If they do go wrong, how would you deal with them?

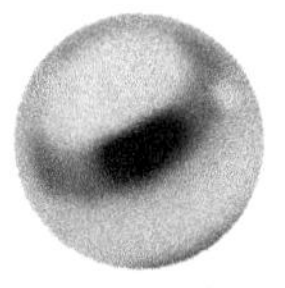

Pearl 61

*Do not
trust people
blindly.*

If someone promises you something, don't just listen and trust it.
Look for system reasons, reality, and
facts that will ensure what they said
is indeed true.

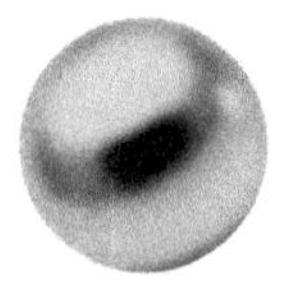

PEARL 62

*Choose
the rare
path.*

Don't crowd in on the road much traveled. It is hard to get ahead, and it does not differentiate you. Identify and travel a road *less* traveled and build your life uniquely.

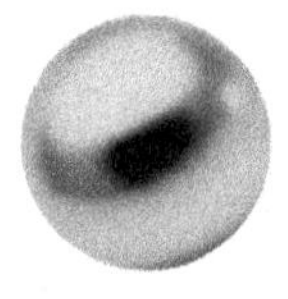

PEARL 63

The 75% Rule—
don't follow
rabbit trails.

When looking at anything, always examine the situation in a majority of the cases (75%). Don't get bogged down with exceptions.

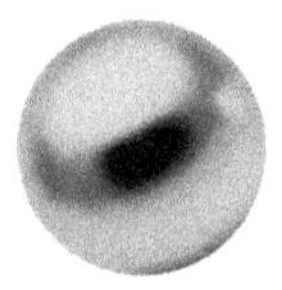

Pearl 64

*Learn why
you succeed and why
it worked.*

When something worked in life, stop, and pause, and contemplate, *"Why* did it work? Are there any lessons that can be learned?"

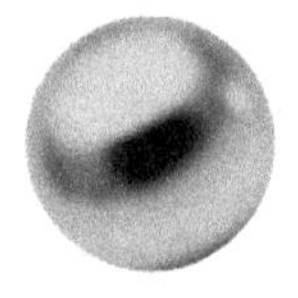

Pearl 65

The best
ideas work.

No matter how good an idea was, move on if it does not actually work!

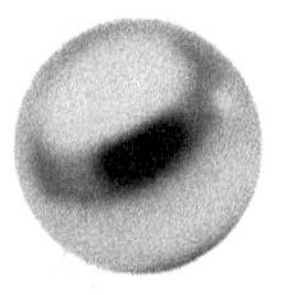

Pearl 66

*Speak in the
language of the listener,
not the speaker.*

The goal of communication is to be understood. So, speak in the language of the listener, and *not* that of the speaker!

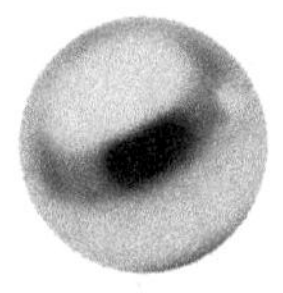

Pearl 67

Investigate all
available choices.

Before making a decision, make sure that you have indeed examined carefully *all* of the available choices. Jumping into making a decision and then finding out that there are actually choices that were not considered, is a waste of time!

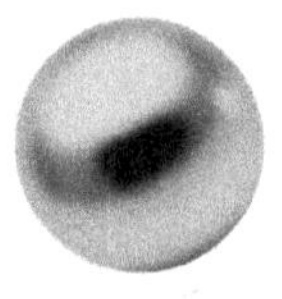

PEARL 68

*Have no
halfway partners.*

Either involve someone in a whole discussion, or do not involve that person at all. A person who does not know all of the factors that apply to your situation will waste your time with unworkable options and irrelevant advice. Involving someone halfway is the best way to create confusion!

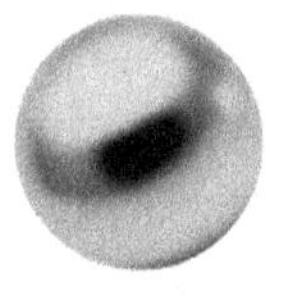

Pearl 69

*Choose the time
to stand
on principle.*

A customer is always right when you are *in front of* that customer. Sometimes, you must choose good will between people over being right. Do your best to balance kindness and correctness.

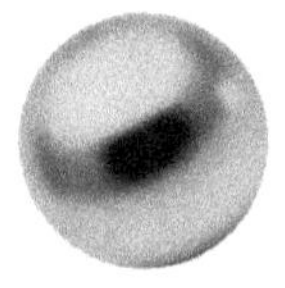

Pearl 70

*The best life
balances
virtues.*

Lack of effort hurts productivity, while extreme effort uses all of our energy and leaves us unhappy. So, *life is always an optimization process.* Finding your particular balance gives you a good life. (If the vertical (Y) axis is productivity or happiness, and the horizontal (X) axis is human effort (from 0% to 100%), then life is always a bell-shaped curve. While 0% effort will get us nowhere (low values in the Y axis), trying while ignoring the writing on the wall (100% effort) is also detrimental and non-productive (also low values in Y axis). So life, is always, an optimization process, i.e., we keep on working and exploring to find that particular location on the X axis (particular % of effort) where the vertical Y axis value (productivity/happiness) is at a maximum).

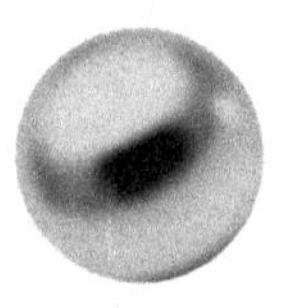

Pearl 71

When evaluating a situation, use BOTH subjective (mental impression) and objective (factual data) approaches.

In assessing a person or a situation, be sure to have *both* subjective and objective info.

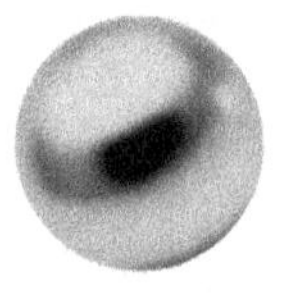

Pearl 72

*Focus on the problem
that you can do
something about.*

When faced with a list of
problems, focus only on the
problem that you can do something
about.

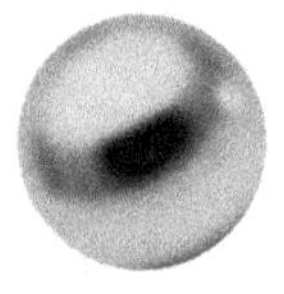

Pearl 73

*People have a
one-track mind.*

$$P$$eople are there for one reason and one reason only. They *don't* pay attention to anything else.

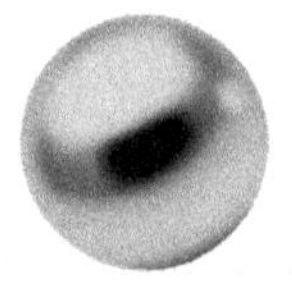

PEARL 74

*What
ultimately
matters?*

W hat ultimately matters, is *not* what you think you said. It is what is understood by the listener.

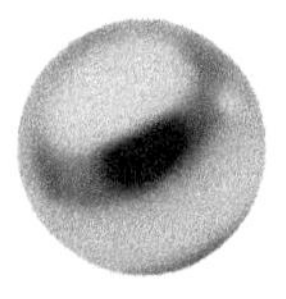

Pearl 75

*Always
think
"Why?"*

W hatever we do, always ask ourselves, "WHY do we do this in this way?"

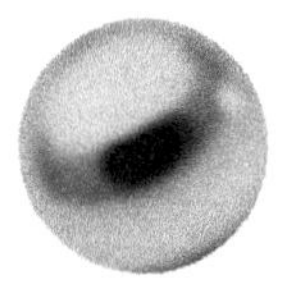

Pearl 76

*Commitment
comes before
"how."*

D on't worry about *how* to do
  something until after you are,
indeed, sure that you really *want* to
do it!

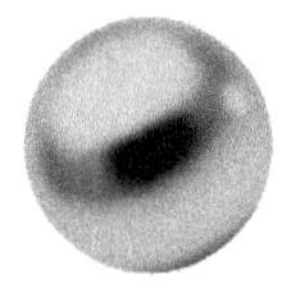

Pearl 77

*What do
you want?*

Life has *less* to do with what it will give you objectively, but *more* with what you want subjectively.

About the Author

Dr. Ming Wang is a Harvard and MIT graduate (MD, *magna cum laude),* and is one of the few laser eye surgeons in the world today who holds a doctorate degree in laser physics. He is the director of Wang Vision Institute in Nashville, TN and CEO of the U.S. division of Aier Eye Hospitals, the world's largest eye group with 900 eye centers on three continents, 80,000 employees, and a market cap of $100 billion.

Dr. Wang has performed over 55,000 laser vision procedures, including on over 4,000 doctors, as well as the world's first laser artificial cornea implantation. He published 10 ophthalmic textbooks and 120 scientific papers, including one in the world-renowned journal *Nature.* Wang Vision Institute is the only center in the state that performs these state-of-the-art vision procedures: SMILE (small-incision LASIK) (18+), Implantable Contact Lens (21+), Forever Young Lens (45+) and laser cataract surgery (60+).

The award-winning film *Sight* (angel. com/sight), the first first-generation Chinese American immigrant film in American mainstream media with a nationwide theatrical release (2,118 theaters), is based on Dr. Wang's autobiography *From Darkness to Sight,* and co-stars Terry Chen and Greg Kinnear.

As a teenager, Ming endured poverty and hardship in China and came to America with only $50. He earned two doctorate degrees—one in laser physics and one in medicine—and graduated with the highest honors from Harvard Medical School and MIT.

The amniotic membrane contact lens, which Dr. Wang invented and for which he holds two U.S. patents (which he has donated to the world), has been used by tens of thousands of eye doctors in nearly every nation in the world to restore eyesight to millions of patients. Today, the amniotic

membrane contact lens is a $5 billion in-
dustry and has transformed the world.

Wang Foundation for Sight Restoration
has helped patients from over 40 states in
the U.S. and 55 countries, with all sight
restoration surgeries performed free of
charge. Dr. Wang was named the Kiwanis
Nashvillian of the Year for his lifelong ded-
ication to helping blind, orphaned children
from around the world.

Dr. Wang also received the Honor
Award from the American Academy of
Ophthalmology, the Lifetime Achievement
Award from the Association of Chinese
American Physicians, NPR's Philanthro-
pist of the Year Award, and an honorary
doctorate degree from Trevecca Nazarene
University.

About the Publisher

Born into a military family in 1972, Robbie Grayson III's upbringing unfolded against the backdrop of Cold War Europe. Commencing elementary school in 1977 (Bitburg Elementary School) and culminating in a high school graduation in 1990 (Mehlingen Christian Academy) in former West Germany, Robbie's formative years were also marked by four transformative years in England (1983-1987). His experiences, deeply influenced by the geopolitical tensions of the era, fostered a curiosity about the world and a diplomatic outlook.

While traveling Europe with his family and attending DOD (Department of Defense) and private American schools, Robbie encountered a diverse array of individuals and witnessed significant historical events. The tumultuous late 1980s, in particular, left an indelible mark, as he experienced firsthand the reverberations of revolution, notably the Fall of the Berlin Wall (1989), the crumbling of Perestroika, and the eventual collapse of Communism.

Following graduation from Pensacola Christian College in 1996 with a B.S. in Elementary Education, a minor in English Literature, and an eclectic concentration in psychology, Robbie founded the alternative education program Stone Table School in Franklin, Tennessee, where he dedicated himself to the minds of Music City's elite youth until 2011. Since then, he has been involved in book publishing.

Robbie has been married to his wife, Sharilyn Suzette Smith-Grayson, a writer and educator, since 1997. Together, they have six children. They live in Franklin, Tennessee—"The Malibu of the South"— where Robbie maintains a grounded presence and frequently can be seen at a Starbucks in the historic district of Downtown Franklin.

The film *Sight* (angel.com/sight) is based
on the autobiography *From Darkness to Sight*
by Dr. Ming Wang, co-starring Greg Kinnear.

Dr. Wang's autobiography
From Darkness to Sight, based on which
the film *Sight* (angel.com/sight) has been made,
is about his journey from China to America
and from hardship to healing.

WANG VISION
INSTITUTE

3D Cataract & LASIK Center

1801 West End Avenue
Suite 1150
Nashville, TN 37203

www.drmingwang.com
drwang@wangvisioninstitute.com

9 798886 919 2943